by Molly Smith

Consultant: Brian V. Brown
Curator, Entomology Section
Natural History Museum of Los Angeles County

BEARPORT
PUBLISHING

New York, New York

Credits

Cover, © Stephen Dalton/Minden Pictures; 4T, © Bob Jensen/Alamy; 4M, © Cisca Castelijns/FOTO NATURA/Minden Pictures; 4B, © Hans Christoph Kappel/Nature Picture Library; 5, © Skip Moody/Rainbow; 6, © Kim Taylor/npl/Minden Pictures; 7, © Michael Durham/Minden Pictures; 8, © F.Labhardt/4nature/WILDLIFE/Peter Arnold; 9, © Szabo Photography/Shutterstock; 10, © Kim Taylor/npl/Minden Pictures; 11, © Stephen Dalton/Minden Pictures; 12, © F.Stich/WILDLIFE/Peter Arnold; 13, © Jozsef Szentpeteri/National Geographic/Getty images; 15, © Ross Hoddinott/Nature Picture Library; 16, © Dwight Kuhn/Dwight Kuhn Photography; 17, © Hans Pfletschinger/Peter Arnold; 19, © Ross Hoddinott/Nature Picture Library; 20T, © blickwinkel/McPHOTO/Alamy; 20B, © Gary Meszaros/Photo Researchers, Inc.; 21, © Michael Durham/Minden Pictures; 22TL, © Gregory G. Dimijian, M.D./Photo Researchers, Inc.; 22TR, © David Cappaert, Michigan State University, Bugwood.org; 22BL, © David Cappaert, Michigan State University, Bugwood.org; 22BR, © Kim Taylor/Nature Picture Library; 22Spot, © Saied Shahin Kiya/Shutterstock; 23TL, © Jim Wehtje/Photodisc Green/Getty Images; 23TR, © Cisca Castelijns/FOTO NATURA/Minden Pictures; 23BL, © Ross Hoddinott/Nature Picture Library; 22BR, © Dwight Kuhn/Dwight Kuhn Photography.

Publisher: Kenn Goin
Editorial Director: Adam Siegel
Creative Director: Spencer Brinker
Design: Dawn Beard Creative
Photo Researcher: Beaura Kathy Ringrose

Library of Congress Cataloging-in-Publication Data

Smith, Molly, 1974–
 Speedy dragonflies / by Molly Smith.
   p. cm. — (No Backbone! The World of Invertebrates)
 Includes bibliographical references and index.
 ISBN-13: 978-1-59716-583-9 (library binding)
 ISBN-10: 1-59716-583-2 (library binding)
 1. Dragonflies—Juvenile literature. I. Title.

QL520.S65 2008
595.7'33—dc22

                    2007041792

For more information, write to Bearport Publishing Company, Inc., 101 Fifth Avenue, Suite 6R, New York, New York 10003. Printed in the United States of America.

10 9 8 7 6 5 4 3 2 1

Contents

Dazzling Dragons

Dragonflies are large **insects** with long, thin bodies and two pairs of wings.

People call them dragonflies because they look like flying dragons.

There are about 3,000 different kinds of dragonflies.

Their bodies can be bright colors such as emerald green, ruby red, or shiny blue.

Like all insects, dragonflies have a hard covering called an exoskeleton. The exoskeleton protects the soft inner parts of an insect's body.

5

Built for Speed

The dragonfly is one of the fastest fliers in the insect world.

Its front pair of wings can move separately from the back pair.

By moving its wings in different ways, a dragonfly can fly forward or backward.

It can also twist and turn or even stay in the air in one place like a helicopter.

A dragonfly can fly as fast as 35 miles per hour (56 kph). That's faster than a person can run.

back wings

front wings

Big Eyes

Dragonflies have huge eyes.

Their eyes are made of thousands of tiny parts called lenses.

Each lens is like a tiny eye.

All these tiny eyes work together to help the dragonfly see in every direction.

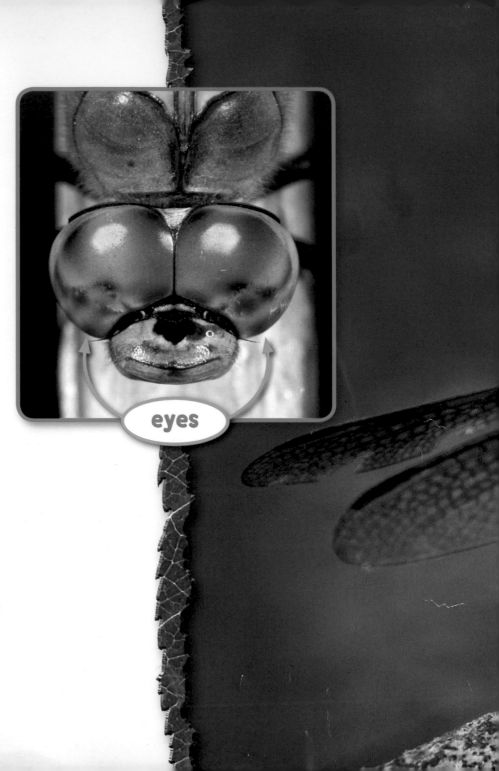

eyes

Dragonflies have the largest eyes of all insects.

8

Hungry Hunters

Dragonflies catch and eat flying insects.

They have two main ways of hunting.

Some fly through the air looking for insects to attack.

Others sit and wait for victims to pass by—and then dart out to grab them.

Mosquitoes, flies, wasps, and beetles are some of the insects that dragonflies hunt.

11

Flying Food

A dragonfly holds its legs in the shape of a basket while it is flying and hunting.

It uses this basket to scoop up insects in the air.

Then the dragonfly uses its strong jaws to eat its victim—all without stopping to land!

spikes

A dragonfly's legs have rows of sharp spikes. They help the dragonfly hold on to the insects it captures.

damselfly

A Watery World

Most dragonflies spend their whole lives around water.

Females lay their eggs in ponds, swamps, and lakes.

The babies that hatch start their lives underwater.

They will spend the next few months growing up there.

Some dragonflies live in deserts and other dry places. They wait for rain or a flood to lay their eggs.

Growing and Molting

Baby dragonflies are called **nymphs**.

Their soft bodies grow quickly, but their hard exoskeletons cannot get bigger.

So the nymphs **molt**—shedding their old exoskeletons and forming new ones.

They can molt up to 15 times while they are growing up.

Preparing for Takeoff

After months of eating and growing, a nymph is ready for its last molt.

It crawls out of the water at night and sheds its exoskeleton.

At first, its wings are wet and crumpled and its new exoskeleton is soft.

By the time the sun rises, however, the wings are dry and the exoskeleton is hard.

The adult dragonfly takes off into the sky.

Once they become adults, dragonflies live for only a few weeks.

adult
dragonfly

old
exoskeleton

19

Dodging Danger

Even though dragonflies are fierce hunters, they are not safe from attack.

Many birds, frogs, and lizards eat them.

A spider's web can also be a dangerous trap for a dragonfly.

However, dragonflies can often escape from their enemies.

Their sharp eyesight and fancy flying help them survive.

Dragonflies have been around for more than 250 million years. They were living on Earth before the time of the dinosaurs.

A World of Invertebrates

An animal that has a skeleton with a **backbone** inside its body is a *vertebrate* (VUR-tuh-brit). Mammals, birds, fish, reptiles, and amphibians are all vertebrates.

An animal that does not have a skeleton with a backbone inside its body is an *invertebrate* (in-VUR-tuh-brit). More than 95 percent of all kinds of animals on Earth are invertebrates.

Some invertebrates, such as insects and spiders, have hard skeletons—called exoskeletons—on the outside of their bodies. Other invertebrates, such as worms and jellyfish, have soft, squishy bodies with no exoskeletons to protect them.

Here are four insects that are closely related to dragonflies. Like all insects, they are invertebrates.

Helicopter Damselfly

Bluet Damselfly

Black-Winged Damselfly

Mayfly

Glossary

backbone
(BAK-*bohn*)
a group of
connected bones
that run along
the backs of some
animals, such as
dogs, cats, and fish;
also called a spine

insects (IN-sekts)
small animals that
have six legs, three
main body parts,
two antennas, and a
hard covering called
an exoskeleton

molt (MOHLT)
to shed an old
exoskeleton so
that a new one
can form

nymphs (NIMFS)
young insects that
change into adults
by growing and
shedding their
exoskeleton agai
and again

Index

Read More

Cooper, Jason. *Dragonflies.* Vero Beach, FL: Rourke Publishing (2006).

Green, Emily K. *Dragonflies.* Minneapolis, MN: Bellwether Media (2007).

Hall, Margaret. *Dragonflies.* Mankato, MN: Capstone Press (2006).

Learn More Online

To learn more about dragonflies, visit

www.bearportpublishing.com/NoBackbone-Insects

About the Author

Molly Smith has written many nonfiction books and textbooks children. She lives with her husband and daughter in Norwalk, Connecticut, where she watches dragonflies dart, dance, and hover in her yard.